GENII OVER SALZBURG

Carl R. Martin

Some of the poems in this book were originally published by
the *Denver Quarterly, International Poetry Review, Monatshefte,
Obsidian II, Pembroke Magazine, Pleiades,* and *WordImage.*

The author is grateful for assistance from the North Carolina Arts
Council and to the MacDowell Colony, where a number of these poems
were written, and to the editors of the magazines listed above.

Library of Congress Cataloguing-in-Publication Data:

Martin, Carl R., 1954-
   Genii over Salzburg / by Carl R. Martin. — 1st ed.
     p.   cm.
   ISBN 1-56478-186-0 (alk. paper)
   I. Title.
   PS3563.A723264G4   1998
   811'.54—dc21   97-51437
                                    CIP

This publication is partially supported by a grant from the Illinois
Arts Council, a state agency.

Dalkey Archive Press
Illinois State University
Campus Box 4241
Normal, IL 61790-4241

Book design by Todd Michael Bushman

for Elizabeth Martin

Nature gives us two genii to accompany us through life. The one, sociable and comely, shortens our trouble-filled journey with its cheerful games; it eases the bonds of necessity for us, and in the midst of joy and levity it guides us to those dangerous places where we must act as pure spirits and lay aside everything corporeal, in other words, it leads us to the knowledge of truth and to the exercise of duty. Here it abandons us, since its realm is only the world of the senses and its earthly wings cannot carry it beyond this world. But then another genius steps forward, a strong-armed genius, serious and silent, that carries us across the dizzying depth.

In the first of these genii one recognizes the feeling of the beautiful, in the second the feeling of the sublime. The beautiful is already an expression of freedom, of course, but not of the sort that lifts us above the power of nature. When it comes to beauty we feel that we are free because sensuous urges harmonize with the law of reason. In the case of the sublime we feel free because those senuous urges have no influence on the legislation of reason, since the spirit acts here as if it stood under no laws other than its own.

from *Concerning the Sublime*
Friedrich Schiller

What holds back the anticipated golden age when truth again becomes fable and fable truth?

from *The Ages of the World*
Friedrich Wilhelm Schelling

Contents

1

2

1

The Vision

The shrill, militaristic scream
Of a bird
Over the Baltic sea
Is as dented, gray
As a warboat's hull, its white wind

Captain's compass, in the pilot-
Cabin console reflecting clouds.
A witch's memory
Of Walpurgisnacht, conjured up.
Needle and ice.

Watchfires at sea are an illusion,
A desert's swill mirage
Spilling into the sailor's eye.
Homeward to port the sickness leans
Off balance like a drunk.

The ropes are fouled
That anchor cloud to sea, gull to ocean
Like wings of Bismarckian gold.
Rain seeds the waters with red.
A corpse like a scarecrow rises into the sky.

Caspar David Friedrich

The incurrence of nettles
Afflicts us at the
Edge of our opprobrium, like
An anomalous sea air
Stinging into depression
With its transparent, jellyfish woes.

Tincture of iodine's
The eye of the sun
At morning or evening
On the unsettled shore
Of sea or mountain, where a man's
A mere sketch.

The footloose freedom
Packed with notions,
Is the artist's reflection,
The artisan's skill,
That creates his mirror.
And I am Caspar, Caspar David.

A Question of Identities

And what, dear sir, are you:
The displaced Roman,
Or the misplaced Schumann;
The stolid iconoclast,
Or the furniture turned blue and surly?

A boat of sea!
A wind of Homer?
As your words sparkle, indecently and wet
Churning in the munificent ocean
Of the watchman's keys
As he walks along black ramparts at night
Of the sea-level fortress.

And my lover waits,
Behind shadows of laurels
Or myrtle,
With the thick nest of trees
In their low row
Rising raggedly skyward.

Der Nachtgeist

In black fir ahead
And on distant mountain ridges
A gestating spirit-light
Grows into a woman.

She eats long, metallic
Fingernails of a dragon
Once pasted on a witch:

Sharp as the train's whistle
At Baden-Baden
Or chafing of wheels
Madly on track.

The nails click
Like fireflies in the brain,
Crack like an old man's boots
Guiding passengers by lantern.

Steam rises
To bath embarking beauty
In the brown heat of the spa,
In relentless time.

Outpost of Vienna

This Romanesque cathedral
With its twin towers
Has a moon between them like a lantern.

Ilsa's bitter waters
Like a baptism
Surround one shining stalk,

One moonlit reed
In darkness
Sea shrank from long ago.

Swelling light
On the black, brackish
Surface:

Inland surveyor
That measures men in slow degrees
As they roll, pitch, and yawn . . .

Like the mouth of Hercules.

That Child

The flame
Of a mountain stream,
Too full of furor,
Flows 'round jagged
Time cut stone
And sloshes between
Its pine-lined banks
Like the face of a fräulein
Changing and changing:
Blue genie, streaked cameo,
Continual waif.

What can I say
To stitch that cry
Got-up in green leaves,
Concealed like a god?
Since childhood I've found
You in forest stones;
Etched secretly
On the frieze of a wooded temple.
Now grief betrays me, bitter
Disgust my warden;
Child that stands watching
Daphne: woods-fountain of Munich.

At Potsdam

What edifice of composed felicity,
Like Sanssouci,
Gazes through a cat's eye
In grey and ochre circles

At the dull simplicity
Of the hypnotic, slowly polished
Sky? Like seeing
Someone's reflection in porcelain.

The cold trickle of a klavier,
Its tremulous sonata
Echoing counterpoint, floats
A narrow stream over the grounds.

Yet it seems a contradiction:
River of the soul
Hidden beneath green mounds,
Low trees, modestly rolling land.

Resolutions of time
Are constantly insufficient, as
If words of Kant
Flow smoothly as dialectic.

Viennese Watercolor, Carved Reliquary

Insuperable mention,
The birch tree my coeval
In the march toward Hungary.

Plains loom forward like grease
In black hair of a saber swinging,
Beer salon, singer.

The river slides through them
Between green hills
And a lavender scent.

What Greek reliquary remembers
The gods, Venus and Mars,
In its ivory breast?

What manner of thing the size
Of a beetle, or tiny spindle?
What crude approximation?

The object's the point,
Layout of affections,
The map of the surface.

The Bone Aesthete

Sweet Alexandra of Bavaria
Thinks she has swallowed
A glass piano.

Its keys are finite
In infinite repetition,
Like the cries of birds
With little glass swords
Being stuck down their throats.

The hammers and skulls
Are made of ivory
("of course, of course")
As well as the crucial cargo.

What is this cargo?
It is the bone aesthete,
Whose hard incrimination
Blazes like a cock
In the morning light.

Her phantom chases her
Through the day,
On the castle staircase
And in the reflections
Of stained glass.

Contrasts: For Ingeborg Bachmann

Austrian poet (1926-1973)

You: misted foghorn,
Wolf howl
In a crevasse,
The land is quiet
But your body is not.

Your blood's metered
Tangled drop by drop
A network of trees,
The puddle of vapor
That lights city lamps.

Its tick is forgotten
While you scream to recall
The bird and the shot,
The cry of the air
Cloistered by iron.

You left like that bird
In a halo of fire,
Bitter black all around.
The saber's twirling silver
The flame of a warm Roman death.

Carriage Boy

What drastic and penumbral
Ode to the streets
Are horses of the coachmen mewling?
Madness of purses, cathedrals
Is not enough.
The moon is eclipsed
In the crescent phase
By a wolf of the trees, pure wisp,
Tenuous gases pursuing his brightness.
Higher up, before toy Jugendstil
Letters arise in the sky,
A man-angel pours a bucket
Of bright elixir, cold doom
Down from the stars
Into avenues of darkness, waltzes,
Where the carriage boy
Sits watching *ghost* dust, amazed:
Brightness in his eyes.

And the liveried question:
Does a coat darker than wood
Embellish night with wonder,
Strong oaks with stories?
What is the boy's
Black profile
To the mistress of leaves,
Knot clucking at his throat,
Mechanically, in the wind?
And who is she,
Wrapped in the green swarm of feelings?

Minor Observances, Unnoticed Deaths

The slanted ephemera
Places operatic insurgents in red-caps,
And tassels.

Light spangles green pine
In the tenuous forest:
No Adamesque folly drawn on the mind's
Mirror under this green law.
In a boy's eye, Psyche
Throws laurels, assigns value, her
Verdant foot crushing the signature of tears.

Outside an elegant flat,
The child waits by a narrow stone column
On which his cheek rests.
And a car drives by releasing its hubcap
Dim but shining in slow gyros
Toward its asphalt grave.

Is there a private language of the cello,
Strings sharp and burning like a harp,
That cuts into the life
Of one *human* orchestra
To separate muscle from air?

I had never longed to meet anything like that.
No Scandian angel:
A fresh purveyor of candor
With a tired smile
Hopeful of seduction,
And the little white porcelain cherub,
Slender, with rough wings of a girl.

I'd thought more of Rossini

As I sat under a poor grape arbor
With patches of paint,
Swinging benches and rusted, black iron.

I'd imagined a door.
It cringed at my thought.
Sometimes elves take it: the door into nowhere.

The Cancer Ward

While Chopin and George Sand
Walk in grass
In a field adjacent to the lawns
In the smudged light of dusk

Paroxysms of angry, unheeled sympathies
Bloom in the name of sunflowers,
And the clematis climbs
Silently in the hayloft.

Once in Albany, New York
I got ill in a taxi after chugging rum;
Threw up in the lounge at St. Agnes School
Where our dates hid me from the nuns.

Pain blossoms like black roots of a tree
Blasted by minions crying
For the hanging resurrection of
Prince Rudolph and Mary Vetsera
From their bloody, hunting lodge bed.

In me, the stark snow
Of words;
The stealing, oxymoronic chafe
Of birds of coal tussling in an icy sky.
I stand, a sick Orient

Evasive as the light is,
Or the blue and golden auroras
Of Carl Nielson, where your scars
Are burned into my flesh.

You're as unwarranted, free
As ivy or heart-shaped leaves
Inflicting cover over fantasy,
And the misbegotten Self.

See now,
Those slurs mean nothing to you;
Hair humid, caring
Beneath signs of starred Norwegian frost.

Come here, stand
Where beds rattle against a cold
Hospital wall, our simile of life;
The quiet sea, skilled as the surgical heart.

The Gods of Trakl

Helian
Is the wet, moss-studded stone
In the forest grove.
Its modesty stands alone
On a rise, its sides enclosed by tall
Or broken trees.

Wild fruit
Unlike the statue,
The persimmon's cracked skin
Is a wrinkled
Yellowish womb.
I cradle it in the wind.

O sick heart
Like a borzoi
Making its rounds, jumping
Beneath the willow
To the sister tune of the wands
The whip, the river.

Morpheus
Winks shut
The opal lid, the oval
Of mother-of-pearl
On which this evanescent scene
Glitters with dew.

Dark Eve

Here are anchorites sunk pale, willing
In the horizon's rising water:
Brides of Caligari
Wandering in a Munchian embrace,
Their lips kissing an egg
Balanced on a tall, narrow flute
                    of champagne.
O witness the dance of the mad
And maddening, Trakl's ghost
Dragoons mere skulls, skeletal
Addicts beneath the frosted barn's
Eaves, groping in stalls each
With a tear of morphine on his cheek.
                    What changes,
What fright death has waiting
Beneath a tall empire's columns.
Not even the shining lugubrious
Green of the Tsar's gift malachite
Lofts the ambassadorial spirit:
For is that what "reaches?"
                    And if,
Stone, smoothed, crafted
Isn't what flies, if wings
Are a loose ethereal apparatus,
Like phlegm from God's lip,
That tubercular Son of Man,
Then we're mere devils, dancing alone.

Common Epistle

Dear Margravine,

In the innocuous garden of usurped
memory are several fallen
stone gnomes with the leering
grin on the dead,
and of course there are the buried
red flowers blooming just beneath
earth in the ephemeral,
imperilled region of the mind
known as "Schinkel's Heroes."

How statuesque, kind, approving
this Olympian netherworld
couched in insults of
toothless Bronze Age vulgarians:
really vines freed from winter's glacial
lock, savage, maudlin
green remnants of Swiss or Austrian
ancients that fasten sharp, crude,
dangerous 'round the wrists.

But forgive this communication,
like those ancestral Celtic "saints,"
for it arises not from
the snaking tools of ambiguous affection
but from that which is precise,
interred deep in capitals of glory.
Thus we share a twin reflection:
unmentionable place of the heart.

Spray of Twigs

The rank dolmen of hypocrisy
Still suffuses the evening light, its windows,
With roseate-orange panels of reflection.

Glasses are raised whose pride
Pierces, reaches far
Toward an earthly, eager maid in the Vienna Woods.

The symbol of a fluted flower
Carved in soft stone above her head, she
Needs no one to free her from her will.

Living caryatids like young Hannibals
Immersed in olive leaves, thick buds of myrtle
Give support not to entablatures and friezes

But to the oval frame
Of her charmed love of children and Etruscan light.
She focuses within. Those muscular gods outside

The spacious circle of her lay,
Mute pastoral of her affections, sit and think
As much as *creatures* can.

For they are pure inventions of the flute
And of the Herculean task,
While she resides here in my heart's keen light.

A Place of Catechisms

Love terrifies when you need
one who hates, despises her love.
A cobra is poised
in the cave of Tristan and Iseult
where cherub-fresh cheeks
and liars tip the chalice; her rubies
Lie on a cool, leopard mat.
What wine of sleepy titanium
pours over her cheek,
her pillow of Lorelei tapestry
woven like Rhine water's
unceasing whisper: its rose stem
dark and prickly with thorns,
bubbling echo fresh on
the dreaming wall. This Venus thread
of naked arts is wavery
with scenes of fret-filled lust.
When *are* we released from *time's*
predestined Elector? His hand
circumscribes the thin medieval
arch of incarved, ivory bodies,
the black atmosphere and fiery hoops.

The Spectral Innocence of Saints

The bestiality of beasts, surely.
A clattering of wooden sticks
Echoes through the old, neglected
Mansion in the night.
Wozzeck, Lulu
Partake of the heart's murder
Like the rushing sound of Viking ships
In a darkened hallway.

The angel is beating her
Head against a wooden doorframe.
Anger chafes the subterranean
Like pectoral fruit. Adam
Playing the gay round
On a dull, steel washtub;
Of the unhappiness of life,
The cruel choices of the God.

And the girl listens,
With the sea spiralling
In her ear under the makeshift
Roof of the moon.
The subterranean hoof
Of the apple . . .
In her nakedness
Extending a metaphysical line
From her navel to her pudenda,
And beyond, to the world of curious gnomes.

For Franz Berwald
(1796-1868) Swedish composer

Animated divertissement of the Swedish
Palace guard, like strict toy soldiers
Beneath an overcast in which the sun
Is caught and held.
So serious this business of the dark,
Of northern skies, uninterrupted calm.

Your music lies across the shoulders
Of a young wife: petty, fierce,
Like lynx fur. She's alone,
Missing her mate.
A cadet sees her from an upper level:
Friendly passion, top hats, carriages

Imposing thoughts upon his architectural
Drawings.
The line of pencil leans like a pyramid,
Capital, protective, though he's still
Yet to know children of this world
In whose room and building shadows

Angles of death, loom harbingers
Of love. Franz,
You proffer a smile,
Snow, cannon, and keyboard;
Yet your lighter side's shadow,
Face turned in my direction, explains it all.

A Cup of Wine

A cracked lip revulses me:
A well brimming with frogs,
It tastes of sour breath and feelings,
Like the village idiot.

Yet I taste it deeper,
Feel the rough fleck of skin
While you stand on tiptoe,
Hair glowing in the darkness.

Yes, I feel you:
A wind in my lungs,
Fjords, sailors,
The motley color of your cheek.

For you know the *night*
As well as I, its lies and sleep
That you induce. Its kiss:
The drug you rub inside my lip.

Rococo Fantasy

On the town tower
The clockface is inscribed with angels:
Soft, effervescent bounties of flesh
In sheer gowns and floating scarves
In the Jovian paradiso,
Flaunting time's metal inscription.

What is this explication of sky
To grim clockwork;
Great, finite cogs
Oiled with minutia of fishlife?

Dark, silent town
In the moon's midnight,
Are there no sleighs on the county road;
No Cissaen maidens with lanterns at corners
Or daughters of Germany?

In this Goethe album I'm suddenly
Stuck in torn pages of engravings.
An emptier clock tower of striated marble,
Black and white, casts
Its tall presence in empty court halls.
I'm dwarfed by all but the curve-bellied drawers
Of a single gilt bureau.

Life will admit no Vulpian mistress, cool of form,
To this one frail and envious heart,
And yet I'm condemned for this "sentimental" life
By great art and artists.

Cruel inhabitors of the Arcadian venue
Post a rabbit at its thicket
Stuck in a trap.
The dark, wild cry is lodged in my head.

Harmonious sister with red hair, thick limbs
That sink into a death,
I can't imitate your teetering dance,
Or sanely will your image away!
Your sinuous ballet sweeps through these halls.

Borrowings from Schubert (And Vienna: Fairest Isle)

The sardonic life of tinsel
Is ensconced within a candle,
A flaming tapestry
Or tall antlers of a stag.

Its fire low as a promenade by the Danube
Near a mud-encrusted dam
And a bridge for strollers: all a native song
By heroic son Bruckner.

They've hung his loyal effigy: salt stubble
Of his cheek not impressive;
His intercourse foolish and imperial
At the feet of young ballerinas.

His pate and cheek are nearly translucent;
His schoolmaster's nose
Sniffs notes. The eighth note
A twig or butterfly.

Salvation's Wraith

Betrothed to silk, white lace
The long wands of the trees
Bend, annoy, as they await
The promenade of bees,
Or the dove's wings
Like petals stained with blood.

In the light woods the stagnant spring
Pools in nascent glimmers,
Cool reflections of a black butterfly
Perched upon the native stone
Like a daughter in mourning.
Back among the living, perched
Here her small feet beneath her
Are stained with black soil
Around the toes.

White dress. Hand supporting chin.
She'll not starve us at the well
Whose maiden spirit's wrist,
Hand extended towards us,
Flows with milk.

The Day in Graz

I hate you pathetic wind,
Your solemn advice
Being nothing
Compared to a loved one's tear.

The song of the trees
Rustles toward me:
A chameleon's key
In the rusted lock

That whistles in the air
Like wind,
And reveals a glimmering hand
Bent like the neck of a swan.

Brass, Teakwood, and Murmur

The marks on her skin
Are inimitable: etched
There by twigs
And the cantering nobility
Of the hermit.

Sand creature herself, her salt
Rolls through me like the sea;
My head the disadumbrated
Belly of her flesh, hair afloat
With invisible antibodies.

Tentacles drift
Where her boat meets
That of the ocean, and the brackish
River pours softly into
Its anomalous Self.

In the tiny waves
Silence stirs filaments,
Underground wigs, spiked
And briny with rust.

So here we meet
My inevitable sister;
Quick tongue of your soul
Impressing on me,
Like limbs, your heartbeat's lieder.

Fallen Estate of a Giant Europa

Idlers derivative of public gardens,
Like hawk faces
Haunt the trees in mid-afternoon:
Faint, amputated visages in webs of haze.

Is that a smile,
An ironic laugh
From the inheritors of evening's terminus,
And the pecking of a crow
To the sad accordion?

Europa, like an empress of Austria
In windblown marble robes, baby-fat face,
Looks over her desiccated subjects:
Magpies and cracked Cupids. Of tiny Cupid

A bow is drawn,
With grapes
And a sky like milk at his feet;
The scar where lightning has broadened
His forehead with black.

A troop of gypsies
Has picked the roses clean of blossoms,
Parading their gilt-spoked wagons.
Off to sell their evening wares
To a dusky peasant town.

There buxom pickers
And gaunt old men, testing,
Bite the hard fruit of existence,
Offering sparse coin against a darkening sun.

Fear of Knowing

New and sinister apparitions co-command
The asylum: a bow of iron, flame
In the arrow, the room's old cupboard.

From a tree hollow
Honey mingles with screams;
Relentless scarab
Like a fencer or pistol, or a snail's
Carapace blued with smoke.

I, lonely citizen, am fearing
The edge of corners,
The quietness of leaves, whiff
Of the coroner in his pallid leather gloves.

Some don't worry, believing
In the tribe where the Rhine
Shimmers under steady sun, a favoring wind.
Loki shivers in his chains, resurrection
A dream. Lorelei attend to the bottom pool.

In the swirl of leaves, hard water,
Is a torrent of angels, rustic and cool.
A woman-child anoints me with laurel
And camphor,
Shroud of love, incestuous kisses.

She hands a red feather
Symbolic of ceremony to still my pain.
Her palm is sweaty, drawn from the beehive
Of peat and honey: that calm well.
Her memories turn blonde. All the world understands.

Divagation on a 'Toy' Symphony Attributed to Leopold Mozart

Are those the elemental boundaries
Of the thrush
Trilling in a summary confusion
As of bird and man:
Prelim of the sterling flute?

I like the formal stance of a musical shepherd:
The dance of a kind of history
A klopping one-step of burghers in a circle,
Noise raised above the sway
Of their practical waistcoats.

To Die Regularly

Too many ancillary confections
Are at the table.

The tweezered insect, the ant,
Sublime breeding of the hive,
Is chocolated with thoughts:

Murder, primarily, succeeding
To the throne.
What delights though are ensconced
In the railings of the semi-rich,
Given over so easily to violence!

The fine leg of the daughter
On the stair. The carved head
On the stairpost.
Royal insignia, pewter arms
Of the Prince-Bishop of Fulda.

My darker body's trapped
In the flashed glass of a Wiener Bronzen
Lamp, like a woodland landscape.
Black tree of bronze supporting our blood,
A hungry spaniel beneath.

Nordgeist

Miserable, obsessive nights
Of questioning,
Like an invoice of darkness . . .
How you honor me with fondling.

The rounded oval of the trees
Is like a dark green gown
Holding invisible fruit, maybe oranges,
Beneath the cradling lull of the wind.

I think there is a spirit:
A thin glass of smooth crystal
Whose song of faint stars,
Beckoning gestures into black,
Protects me.

But the how and why,
The necessity of this journey
Is not revealed;
The fullness of her presence that holds
But never answers.

Weimar Rococo

"Sturm und Drang" of young Goethe echoes
In elf trumpets of the cool, elaborate
Mirror on its axis. Rustling red velvet
On a bedstead. Hymns of seduction
Caught for our surprise, trading ivories

That we are told unfortunate by a guiding
Authority. In spring or winter the banner
Unfurls like a leaf carved from dark woods,
Ineffable spirits, as of Daphnis and Chloe.
Mercury an angry spirit, staring at *us*.

The Sin

Sufferings of the wolf,
The crutch of yellow moon
In night's silent, relentless blank
Is an old wives' tale
Full of tree, rock, and hidden maid.

A cowering Madonna
She is the cradle of stone
For water in its stream.
Her luck is nocternal light
Draping her body.

She's pure spirit
So chilled with innocence
That a baby forms, floats,
Speaking the language of tongues;
The slow drift toward truth
Like a snail on a leaf.

Traveling Beauty

The wind so chill is luminous
As a swan, who glides invisibly
In a sunless sky;
And in the gray reflections
Of the park, rain-drenched leaves
Tip gently in a pond.

Citizens in hats and overcoats
Do not crease the midday calm
With business talk,
Of bread, ships, or autos prodded
Along like cattle on
Shiny streets.

The troubling Berlin mob's here
Not the topic, as it usually is
In this superior city;
But in the poet's mind, birds click
Like castanets, around the wrists
Of a dancing gypsy.

On Beethoven's Eighth

Toward idealized form
Life's confusion
Spills its apple, grape seed
And rotten cores;
Inscribes them on the saturnine
Forehead of a dream.

Like the tapping of slag
By Etruscans
From the ore, music brightens
Dragging its slaves
Toward bleeding pits
Beneath arms and chest
Of the dying Gaul, and his moustache
That's tasted last grain.

This gray becomes the sky
With wispy fingers
Reaching across wild wheat
And lakes,
Spreading the blood-red stain
Of the Mediterranean
Even into the stones.

"Two Music-making Genii"

O sweet salient cherubim
Fondling your
Trumpets of morning,
Awaken the bells;
Unfurl cloudy satins
Above the high spire
In regnant skies.

Conversation

Ides of enmity, anguish, grief
Or some collected strife,
As from a dish of pennies;
Was this Schumann's "Spring,"
That vast, evanescent scoring?

The budding catkin, tall willowware
Of maids: the one with the light
Porcelain basket that sheds
A burst petal of flame
In the still feline's eye.

Yes, it's as simple as that
I think, not calm, redundant
Plain as banished Eusibius.
Someone whispering to us in the dark
Room with the tiger-spotted lily.

Jupiter Flower

After Mozart's "Jupiter" Symphony

The chided blossom
Is like a smoked perfume
From which a glass formed of wishes and desires
Elevates its figure upon the girl's thoughts.

Fleur-de-lis,
Like palm-crossed designs mapped on the metal
Of the back of brush or mirror
In slight molten valleys, rills,
Trumpets chivalric ardor in soft effusion
Near the glow of the still young face.

Is that the fire that burns like brush
Among the tender wails of children
Whose voices chant her evening?

But we never return
To earliest apprehension of a fate.
That is what turns on mental wings
Inside the mind she nourishes with song.

The tardy days will pass us by
Like water over a sudden fall: short, steep
And sudden.
Bent over rocks she stares,
And there is no reply but birds.

Sweet singers of the mellifluous page
Lifted up from Eve or glen
Beyond the ivory chatter of the past
To reflect her like a mirror that looks at us.
She stares, naked, swiftly exposed;
We taken by the protuberance of a rose.

Enigmatic design of natural things,
How can we encompass life as you?
Gentle and good, productive and free,
You seem our opposite, unless cold, we're exposed
   in you.

And now, through slow withdrawing distance
Removed, we see her shiver in a forest breeze,
Water about her feet
As her vision seems to fade from us, imposed.

I fly like hawk or oriole over fields
Of hay, the jupiter flower
Glistening soft and blue. One eye piercing sunlight,
The other struck in the clouds.

Thomas Mann in Crisis

And how did I obtain this lecturing,
Monocled self on an imagined leash,
When that boy
That beautiful boy,
Educated in some way I'd enhance,
Carries his yoke from town to town.

O gypsy class of youth:
Pugilists, wearers of style,
Like farm boys on their tavern walk
To town whose "uncorrupted" hearts
I might taint, like the Nazi decadent,
You tempt . . .

While my inner eye
Thinks Hans Castorp a more suitable sort,
And Clavdia, at first like a fugitive
From the Ballet Russe, has bore my own
Foreign offspring, who put a scare
In the pupils' splintered black

And promise in the Pringsheim way
More stark and truculent fear to come,
Both *Royal Highness* and *Black Swan*
That lazy pipes, conversation,
And summer whites have spawned.
My solitude not fit.

My glass interjects this trouble,
This self-sceptical, barely temperate
Heat, beneath lines that wonder
If I wear "Papa" well, though that
Has the ring of silent satisfaction.
Luxury, luxuriant rebuke.

What can I afford: black to serve,
Or the Word to set me in place . . .
Astute, impressive boys to light my way?
Pretence is something, cuddled in its arms
Raised in discretion what harm can I do?
The mirror, however, still winds its clock.

But no, I have no part in my tales:
Abstraction, particular and cold, sets me out
In some critics' view.
Thomas Mann whose *Magic Mountain*
Couldn't be seen or blasted through,
Though the levelling best was done.

And that's called "the common weal."
So I'll keep my bourgeois airs, stay
Ensconced in *littérature's* aristocratic cradle.
My crisis of flesh waits out its tenure
Of birth and death. Of waiting
I know as much as the eternal Lorelei.

Child on Painted Vase

The world's agog with use
Like a saint's patrimony.

Here swells salvation
In the bent peasants'
Dusty recriminations

Stinking carts of manure
Or violins
Of Bremen's donkey musicians.

Bread and Circus flows
Even in bone-ridden catacombs;
Martyrs attuned to God's lone rhythm:

It sounds like a beggar
On one good leg, or an idiot-child
Lilting toward gilded clouds of bronze.

Black Night

As Brunhild and her sword rise shining
Through the depths as from the sky,
Lament is forged as if, like opium,
It were a law of steel.

Gold shield confounded
By flocked seaweed, heavy bracken
Beneath tides of cold, black ocean,
Blossoming sweetmeats of the sea.

Gilded carnivore
Slither under invisible oars.
A clownlike, sarcastically smiling Charon
Has the head of Osiris balanced on his palm.

O Venus, St. Peter!
Stars are cripple fingers of the dew
Which creeps down to cover us in a wash
Of frightening tints and feverish coughs.

The turgid slap of water
On the little hull feels like a stone,
A gasp for air,
An arbor *inversely* reflected.

2

Poem for Rita
Niece of Dr. Christiaane Barnard

All is darkness,
or, still to come, the intent
of beauty expired
in human felicity . . .
woman's sad child
in the oval mirror of tears:
and the bird cries
in its last soaring,
"too late the phalarope!
for I am but a figment . . . mankind,
noble, mute, in flight:
of breath's care, the last chime."

Two Wishes Stolen from Two Girls

(1)

Two sparrows
Like quail in the summer deliquescence
Have chucked it all into the wind,

Have vomited unacknowledged
Into the pool of Being.

Can I tell Marta that I will not
Seek St. Francis in a distant inner life,
Even naked beside her while others
Pretend to sleep, but rather weave this tapestry
That tells of nothing unto nothing?

How silent it is:
The cloaked bell tower; the unalienable citizen
of the irrevocable Death.

It glides on Venetian waters
Past sullen dripping of stones
Into the house of the taximan, where
Breads are little pellets
Among fire, dogs, and Flemish pots.
The long oiled hair of his daughter
Whose eyes shine at you undaunted.

How rapturously the plague
Will ferry her, cloaked under
The dark bubble of his presence,
Through the black canals at night.

(2)

Inviolate cadre of dominating feathers,
You sit so easily in your round-bellied vase.
Why couldn't you be a woman, pregnant,
Or with the smooth hard belly, flat
As the surface of a stone from the stream?

She need fear no fist from me.
Nothing to cloy the passage.
To make her stomach ripple to the touch
And she convulse backwards, laughing.

You make her an enemy with the clock;
Black passing of hours in her apartment.
The hallway dark with scent, dead memory.
Aunt and other family, inhabiting nowhere.
The tense, accustomed city making street sounds.

Her arms slump over her dressing table.
Brown face in the mirror reminding her
Of Sicily, Naples: barefoot, stepping
On the ground—her earth, her place.

Vermin

The corsair of Rembrandt
Like a coven of mustangs,
Looses cannon
Against the crackling, revolutionary sky.

Divisions of the navy
Are a still bat
In the closet with sword
And skull.

Fly, fly people!
A cord of red strangles
The neck vein of the idiot,
Enemy of the country.

And all not lost
Suffers transmutation,
Metaphorical egress;
Inn of the caterpillar, scarving the dead.

Pierrot, Harpie, and Landscape

The costumed polonaise that carries me
Through ramparts of water backed by the moon
Has its girl yelling, "Metaphor, metaphor!"
As a kind of critical incidence; alliteration
Of voices.
The wrappings are ghostly by the blue roots
Of the ocean's delicately drawn tree,
Where she hovers like a small, distraught fog.

Ah Voltaire, neophyte of the candid appraisal,
Mocker of the vain temple of flesh,
In woods the wrought iron is crumbling,
The gold tint bleeding off the sun.
Your mansion is visited by cold and wood sprite.
No fashionable cane marks the winding path.
Pangloss a painted and *sorry* ensign . . . by the
    diplomatic creek.

The Cult of Language

Dense coagulations of sound
Splinter black lights
Underwater: falling
Of bells
Through scars
And curlicues,
The squiggly semen of seaweed.

Pulsating nodules
Erect with filaments
Wave from a mushroom surface,
Hooked to the flagellant broom
Drifting up like tiny stalks
From the ocean floor.

The orphaned face
Of Jane Eyre stares
From an ocean cameo,
Huge and interested as Artemis.

From the shell of the moon
Filtering down
Come voices
Stinging like nettles in a wind,
Webbed like flax
In a slave graveyard:
Chimeras at noon.

Popilla Japonica: Japanese Beetle

What winded protest
Like a bloody earwig scraping
His appendages
At the supplicating door,
What chalk dilemma perpetrates
A girl's voice through time's black
Room? Are these my cry,
My diminished craft
That floats on wings of dust
In a sullied lake?

The Presence of Snow

Don't you understand
Sign language fool, said the
Girl to the fool who raised
A metal crutch, her eyelids
Thin as birch the effervescent
Tree with a parched skin
Of snow, just like the eland
Has migrated to Iceland
Trotting and shaking his horns,
And the fool fell at her feet
Like a seeing eye dog chewing
The skin of an orange.

East

The tired, abused tide
Of custom is a tent of huskies
Each front paw raised in frozen
Dance in Siberian snow.
Umbrellas fall in the blizzard
While violin and jew's-harp
Play their strange sonata
Where there's no one at all,
But the shadow of Pushkin
White with contemplation.

The Changeling Roan

That beast of conveyance
Or trotted-out clemency
Strikes with stars the deep blue,
The candle in the cavern
Of its mother's mouth
Where the wind is nil, red
Tongue nil. Clouds blow
Black in the changeling roan
Of tree and cloud, boot and plow
And the plowman's brow,
In the rolling cart of the roan's mouth.

"We All Crazy Sam"

Dogs have died their bitter death
Following the leaves and
Hemlock of the acerbic elves;
A black wind from the bole.
Car-shaped balloons are waylaid
Flattened home to Miss Droom's School.
Picked clean by long, interesting fingers
For bad wasps nesting in the eaves:
Crown of thorns
In the dustball's loony bin.

Love Poem

The ancient crater lake is
Brimming with burning volcanic
Letters formed in its gray
Sky by flocks of bees.
This isn't true, but
Neither are you, dear,
Budding phlox, piece of work
Wrought from flesh. You're in my
Limbic system, and your
Soul slumps out at me like
The lingonberry tongue of a cow.

Untitled

Dark purveyor of deeds
To what transgression
Do seed and woodcock aspire
That you cut deep
Into the mouth of wheat
Whose sweet tongue roils in the black?
Stutters wound like an axe
That ghost of a self
Who lives in the wood.

The Dog That Fertilized Heaven

The crypt of soup on which
The yellow butterfly skims
Is dashed with salt
Like effluvium on a pond of scum
That tipped the hat of the man
In the purple skates who icing
Was cruelly exposed to
The pink belly of veils
Underneath her spring shower
Where the dog shat
Kissing the daylight moon
Singing celadon, potash & caveats.

King Frog

We are correct in the naming
Of frogs who in curt elevation
Croak from the trees; Baby
In swaddling clothes, darkness
Removed from his tongue like
A curdle of smoke as he hears
The song of the Stilson wrench
Sung by the train engineer,
While the tears of frogs
Are drops of crystal:
Snakes' eyes in West Virginia.

Local God

We pray to this spirit
Who eats us,
Eats us like worms.
He eats us.

In dark he sleeps
In the mamba's dream,
Becomes a green snake
Who dances in the fire.

Nothing can shake him
If he wants to kill you
But the water of dream,
The witch doctor's rattle.

What the Dictator Found

Lisping grammars, putative cats and dogs
And the pervasive symbol—the station wagon
Couched in a kind of dissent.
Why were ghost children
Spitting out flaming amorphous
Sunseeds in the captivating
Rigors of mourning,
On the way to a last day
Of school? Tracks
Eaten by the scent of monkeys,
With heat filtering
Off crumbling edges of asphalt
Slick with tar and oil;
Piscine dreams of club salmon
Vomited out.
Susan, the oldest child,
Struggles to speak, and nothing
Comes but a cottony tolling of anger;
A drowning, choked feeling
As a giant moth's
Born out of her mouth:
Dusty, death-aged wings like a burst
Pod of milkweed: nauseating thing emerging
To leave her stark as the light.

Anna Akhmatova, You Have Sinned

With you hidden under
A canopy of black sable
A star shines through a
Furry bullet hole.
No more dancing by
The sea, no more dancing
You have sinned, you have
Sinned; from the Oder
To the Baltic
You spread your white wings
And splintered the eye
Of the Volga boatman
Into colors and songs.
Where white waves
Touch the shoreline
You have smothered his cry
By those sandy shores.

You have punished
The children. You have
Punished their laughing.
Your cold, entrancing
Eye has punished
Their laughing,
On the shores of the street.
Your lies smelt the oar
That powers the sun:
Sparking its strokes
Into palaces of light.

Sensibility Shaped by Blood

Piquant ambitions
Lave the moldering succession of the tides.
A newborn ship,
Sail tilting toward the dense corporeal
Shore,
In the orange dusk.

Crepe curls of Portsmouth
Worn out of the tired, lanky hair
Of urchin hopefuls.
Bearing a chest of dreams, a broken doll,
One clutches at a rope,
Standing on dirty sunburned toes,
Into serfdom all her hope charmed, coiled
Like a snake,
But black, black as a storm.

A slave is staring
At the nihilist sky;
Into struggle born he sees a future clear.
A dreary bell whipped into a frenzy
In calm disported clouds of darkening hue,
A silent bell, invisible to sense.

A rider galloping, galloping
In the darkness; a rogue's dagger,
A lady lately fallen, clutching her heart.
What say you Raleigh now
Out of that holy land,
On your last bead: you laugh the executioner's
    curved, grinding axe.

A Close Thing

These classic interruptions
Gleaming glissandi
Like maidenhair attached
To the stone under the stream,
Flow from havoc reeds;
Bubbles gliding up, bursting
Near the stalk.

Three Graces tend the wind
From broom and asphodel;
The bobbin that climbs the loom
Of sunlight
Whispering, "Emily, come down
Come down,
The bell in your chapel's
Broken now.

The spider will no longer
Frighten you."
But zephyred, golden maidens
Turning in their circle
To her key,
As by a musical deus ex machina
Still do. She puts its marble
Circle base
Back on the mantle.

X2.1

The ethos immobile
Of the personality,
Like a sculpture in a glass totalitarian,
Does not move to the tone of the music,
Nor calm pervade the whole.

Questions of possibility
Like bubbles explode from the center,
As if intellectual history remained
Intact as inquiry. Molded to form, what mind
Is set in enclosed space whose borders
Are not squares?
What memory professes the heart derides,
Preferring nemesis of care in mimetic
Cures, whose calm pervades, allures.
The God of time whose music curves,
Plays with the actors' Sunday speech.
A house of numbers from podium built
Before the child knows guilt.

Dull balloon that rings in space:
Without cares, my wish is yours,
Belongs to April in the school
Where many children are set aside,
Strip for monkeys in a room
Where brass listens at every side.
A waiting room for those who die.

And in that apathetic speech,
Of one, autistic, on the grass,
Does the pale distance play his tune
Of trees, school, and bridge over stream?
Will he meet the genius in blocks of wood
To turn and overturn the lady's hand
In another . . .

Another *waiting* room. She'll have soft
Strawberry blonde hair
In wisps of errant, unprofessed care.

Names,
Names will have it.
They will have *us*.
Or who will have us
In the end?

Daimon of life, child of the sun,
Near to your heart you fall and run;
And I stand aside, with glance
Deep away, and into the stream hold total sway,
For I'm but a moment no child may say.

Where It Is and the Colorless Rainbow

The skein of night
Like tiny modules of water,
Drops in the skeletal frame of time:
An accident of the last enervated kiss,
The last awakening limb.

Contortions of an empty street,
One small frame house, lost in the play.
A play house, the twisted hemisphere;
The naked contusions,
Bleeding with kisses, like broken glass.

And you ask me to say
Where
I was dipped in that clear place
Of her voice,
Laying blame to every jerky tension;
The spittle that dropped on an arch
From a laugh;
The imperfections of teeth and sweat.

The laugh on a Saturday
That broke through our cartoon
Of unprepared remorse.
Each single loneliness of sunshine
And preparation for the bath.
The strand of hair gleaming
By the white towel,
By the chipped porcelain bath in the window's
    light.

And the light seems pierced by an arrow
Dividing my brain in limbo,
In sharp refractions of near darkness.

Just Another Bearish Downsweep

Soldier marionettes
Of an ineffable solicitude
                 now infest
The margins
     of predictability
Concuspicient mouths like oranges
Epaulets of gloomy lipstick-red
The nominee
Is lost in a summer nest of bees
Sun casting bright shadows
Through the reflecting word
Of leaves.

The hobnail
Exposes its rusted face
Flat, brilliant, unseemly as politicians
While it referees
Audits the sole of defining sand,
                 Fish glint
As through a sieve
Of sifting, immobile thought:
A porcelain brooch
A foot lost in a factory

Lincoln, Hoover, the whole damn brilliant
     bunch,
Like flowers on a lapel;
The dried aftermath, investors howling
Through leaves in a strangely sinking clearing.

The Exegesis of Flowers

Well . . . this must begin in earnest,
Not vague as poppyseeds
And teacups, and the color of the sky.
Oh yes,
Especially no doyenne roaming
Through these profound, unleavened
Corridors of heaven; manses
With observatories tinged with blue
Gunmetal fevers
Of the past,
Erupting oiled through the fancy
Cracks of clouds.

This long arch of silken petal
Drawn out against
The darkened envies of the sky,
Produces tweaking blanks of pollen
To fall and multiply.
While dim Darwinian corporals
Of black night breathe searing spores
Of powder. The sparks of fire
Flare distantly, near cold
Ways of destruction by the snail.
We corrupt children of the night
Milk a broken stem like ants,
Demanding due of every 'thing'
We foster.

A Miniature of "The Children's Rebellion"

Odes of lush counterinvention
Scrambled through the weeds
Like kids
Tunnelling through
To a clubhouse of painted slats,
Bare earth, one wall of sun.

The Provencal murmur
Casting aspersions
Naughty as summer dizziness
Or the tops of sunflowers
Spread by word of vine;
The swinging, clutching ropes
Of pirates.

This was the new style:
The integral approach.
Stuffing the apron with straw,
Putting flowers
In the spouts of porcelain.

And finally the buzzing bees,
Or the lily's incisions around
And into the one soul by the pond,
Wore the badge of infants:
A silly smile,
The sleep whose shadow
Creeps slanted, over the cot
At noon.

Strange

The privilege, the touch
Is circumspect.
Incursion to the root of many bushes.

What sin maintains this moist Youth,
Childlike memory of things
Flowering elemental,
This institute anything but virgin.

And yet the chaste roots
Rise straight into the tree
Beside the white, limestone facade.
Chiselled form: shadow, leaf, and bark.

The self, the visible self
Or "mystery of self"
To dog the child's sensual simplicity
As he imbibes the word, "responsible?"

An early cross to bring
To naked, forest dreams: the woman
Curled in dark, universal cloud.

The sperm flies up,
A wild, unreckoned, uncontrollable
Force
Changed into breathing spirits.

On the Allusive Pleasure of Modern Arts

The proscribed cinema,
The elusive sunbeam,
The coup de jouet:
All versions of the imaged wall, bricked,
Alight with the sun
Like a kind of cool Stella,
The water vibrating beneath it
And faintly overcast by ivy.

You are more richly figured,
Unlike the geometric sun
That has no sloping curve except
In mind: the elastic chic
Bare of all but skin;
Shaded: a Renaissance appearance
    of the moon.
Looping figures dance these days
Stripped to their bare appeal.

The crypt of a Pharaoh
Imitates our shadowy attitudes.
Or yours, a Celtic tomb
Where a beam of light eeks through
Directed to a spot of rising spirit,
Like sun soaking darkly into skin.
You rise like a strange cross
Amidst flanking leaves and vines.
Your father hardly pays for
All your sins; cultivates fidelity
In a future death.
The sheets are cured in the sweat
    of being,
The pure lick of your hair spread
Dark and thick with life.

Compassion

Convulsive deliverance
In the opaque, milky
Complexion of advertising;
Of soap, of oil
Of the agate rings on the dusty snake.
Orchids bleeding onto garden stones.

Through creepers, pergola,
Necrophilia of alert,
Buddha sits Svengali wise
As pine needles stir a girl's
Naked foot:
The game of light, defending itself.

New emperors
Killed for the fitful release,
In confidence of
Pastors, mistresses, whores . . .
In the fountain of blood.
Day of atonement.

Rare roses canker
In the flow the bloom
Of subjective thought,
Now nailed to a cross.
The fragile jaw
Detached by a blow.

Balloons Empty of Meaning

You're full of empty meanings:
Cruets of sand,
A long, purple face
Spotted with bumps and grain;
You float like a barge on the Seine.

Riven surfaces,
The reflection of a hawk,
Ripples death's mirror.
Your woman,
Divided, loving blood,
Is a presence caught on a shoal
Between sea, sandbar (and word),
Screws turning in vain
Through illusions of light.
Her mask is gold, like a sermon.

The harmonium and monkey,
His jeweled *skull*,
Are alive and well.

And the little toy casket
Of building blocks
Waits for you in the simmering grass.

Knowing the Truth

It is all prepared.
The scaffold like contraband,
The leering teeth
And black tights of female dancers:
Arms, legs enfolded by pink lace,
The heads by white netting.

Why this scarecrow existence,
The piano notes
Like a guillotine in the wind?
Too many presences
Haunt the soiree
And the empty salon, like crystal.

The glove is a mask.
Her hand a deliverance,
As if windmills waited
With their cruel chop and sting
That could always be related
Back to kindergarten . . .
The primary setting
Amorphous with universal
Relevance: the girl
Down whose back you dropped
The snake.
Bare space, pink goosebumps.

And there's the water
Over which truth blows,
Ethereal willows drooping in it:
The slap missing you, over and again.

Where Am I Distant?

Like a conveying walkway in an airport
The stillness is a pebble dropped in water
Whose splash rising in examined globs and spots
Threatens to engulf me in vision.
I stand far away, moving, looking down.
I pass by two small, blue plastic shoes.

I look through glass all around and if
They're there people seem so distant
They correspond only to noises
Like the clicks of a bead game:
Clear glass counted in seconds, two falling
Against one another, over and over.

On the street a yellow taxi
With its meter counting.
And the day stops
In the chill of a glass-gray silence,
While a red apple pouched in clear air
Is somewhere in the incessant green.

Another Kind of Traffic

The red balloon is etched on cerulean
Columns made of sea,
Rising in the updrift
Toward the spume of wavery sky, unethical cloud.

Moping vendors, stockbrokers
Slick executive ladies taut as a watch
Spring, huddle in reflective water.
Glass buildings, stultifying panes
Beam shine, hot momenticular blindness;
Girdered shades
As sticky as a knife point's many feet,
Ignorant as the backdoor lover
Carrying his restaurant's tray of lies:
The ineffectual fervor
That bends her into astrological signs, untoward
    approaches
Dense as the jet's stream, gray with heat
    exhaustion.
Blood pumping, cold pushing inside the body's
    glamorous

Veins, inveterate sweat; the wisp of syllables
Piercing deep into the body like a needle.
Self-hatred painted pictures in the head
From many betrayals.

The cab departs, the shame is multiplicity
Of emotions
Shoring, in truth, upon the native deeps.

A Thinking Reverie

Through instinctual modification
Alcestis squanders the beach ball
Pushed up the hill, Picasso
Gratis Freud,
Mathematical probability
Of the Seine's bank of sand,
And the artist pissing outside
A phone booth.
Contortions make her two-faced
But attractive in a kind
Of bullfight sin
Brechtian cabaret.
Still black-and-white piano notes
Are propagated in the wind
Of which Renoir partakes, and
The attempt to transmogrify
The shape of a brown test tube
Into scarifying creatures.
What we imagine is true
Is true: dark parlor,
Or the garret
Full of glass animals on shelves
That aren't animals
But bugs in a vacuum
Imitating the human.
Speech obstructs like a foreign shadow
Pressing itself between a lover's thighs.
The argument's discursive
In its abstract intuition: a girl
Beaming like the constitution
Of a elephant feeding itself
On the snakelike rhythms
Of tubers.

Smiles are precursors

Of the dinosaurs, as if she
Were stretching, feeling the crack
In the bone,
Measuring a tendon in her calf.
I have calibrated this elixir
With tuning forks,
Found it the average thing
Like wisps across the mouth;
But experience lies
And can be recalled at any point
To verify a rocky earth,
Dark asperities of wine.
French methodology
Is like a Trailways bus and
Is scarce in its tendency
To communicate.
This is simple as seasons,
As the ocean weight shedding
Light . . .
Though impersonality
Is leavened
By red lipstick of kisses.

Studying simian deliverance
(So she says).
A vale of gillyflowers
In the piano study
With beams, shadows, lends
No more to moralism
Than momentarily
The open blouse
Of the music teacher, actress
In its employ.
Divisions exist
In the replication of shadow
And light where the child
Can hide.
Notes, countermeasures

Bisect
The open window that shrouds his eye.

Sullen converse typified
By convoluted scars
In the child's brain
May make the realm of his maturing.

Do arabesques, obelisks
Take human place
In muted static of dusty sunlight
That floats, pools in weird lies,
Inverted shapes of wights?
Dwarves correspond
Like lily pads in a pond
To the sundial's shadows
In the garden,
And they settle 'round legs
Of coffee tables,
Or shimmer
Drifted onto tapestry
Of patterned wallpaper
Stripped from walls
Of an old chateau.
Ivy has attacked
The pergola of grapevines,
Opera of boyhood sweetness
Seeping from books
Where the heroine
Captures the impresario
Of Paris or Vienna with a pure voice
Lifted like limes or ivy
Among Greek statues, myrtle.

Now old songs from Schubert or Delius
Excoriate the center of the orange,
Prime the rooster with gasoline.
Carnival darkness is infused with rouge

And Holsteins, tutus and death.

I can stand that, the sweat
And the puckering
And the schoolgirl's black
Raincoat even darker with age,
Though she's fought me
In covert ways that can't be reconciled.

Toward what motion,
What movements,
As in *Der Fliegende Höllander*,
Do the particles in the piece
Signify attrition of fluid hand,
Metallic stars
Of microscopic invention
Where the polished speculum
Investigates statistic
In private centers for disease control?

The anxiety of 'confluence' shakes me
From my hammock, drops me in a mound
Of leaves. The line is broken,
The rhetoric of poetry, fini.
The Greek mould was never broken,
The "Triumph of the West" is in bed.
Next Italy, the triumph of the best,
Is in sophisticated lies that try
Entangle me. The "naked" artifice,
Sprung rhyme
Bronze and smooth as any bangle.
Dylan Thomas throws up on the bed
(Watch the language, it can lie)
Filching like an eagle the native's cries.

Lambent correspondence of light
Shakes tears from the eyes
Of an old man assuming

'Miltonic blindness' . . . scraping
Butter on the long loaf,
Sourdough face of his wife
Carved from an Alsace quarry
As if Deutsch might
Spurt out at any moment.
At 17 at the Université de Paris
My African friend P.
Consorted with French girls,
As well as I;
Gave some support to a homeless
American hippie pair
Buying her flowered dresses.
All too typical some'd say.
Her husband and I agonized
The situation over wine, he wanting
To drown the stain with absinthe,
Try the hallucinogenic worm
Of Baudelaire. For them
No passport, work permit, fun,
But later, on the verge of eve,
His wife Loretta and I
Giggled and played footsies
In company of graduate students
Under the umbrella of a cafe
While he shushed and screwed
His face to shut us up.
His selling hash for the Moroccans
Was funny business to some French
And with only a university bathroom
To sleep that night.
Without possessions one becomes possessed
With the frequency of fire and death,
The line of fire *as* reported.

Zeno, Alcestis
The realm of paradox. We go swinging
Through the "doors of perception"

Into the salon where Medea has been
Spurned but not disgraced
By our robed girl, Alcestis.
They all like it here
The Free French and the Vichy
In these clothes of France.
The bronzes and champagne
Have been paid for congenially
By Marshal Petain
And the nouveau riche. I have won
Her by yoking a boar and a lion
To the chariot of the sun.
Her legs statuesque,
Thigh right off the vine
Hanging, moving, over th' other leg,
Waiting for that final conflagration.

Someday I *will* mature, nuclear
In all the senses.
"She gave her life that Admetus
Might be spared. But she did not
Remain long in the Underworld."
Kissing, feeling her now,
She yields; the human constitution's
My defense.
The boar, in time, fell like Icarus
From her sky, by
Building sickening constellations
Of the spear.

Generalities infer
Like the furor of fire
The beast of the industrial whirlwind
Behind, ahead.
Colors of light
Like whirring scratches of chalk, gray
Over the blur of people,
Buildings, pool of concrete.

The Trojan horse of empires
Napoleon could not tame or conquer
On his steed.
We fall back into letters.
The Gallup pole feeds us in our circle
Of hell's confusion.
Benares crumples under white sun
Like a sheet of figures
Thrown in the can . . . bleeding;
Black ghosts of Dante superimposed
Over reality in the chalk inferno.
Thoughtfully
Like a cockroach sunk in the heart
Of my refusing Beatrice
I reckon black holes of Calcutta,
But an English rock star wrote me,
Said she wanted to meet me.
Her father makes sure her career's
Not vulgar, but cool
With that young, attractive
British fat.

What you term aimlessness is "art."
Look at the body of the thing:
Full up with breasts . . .
The casual robing at some chic store
Catering in bangles to the rich
In a classic, provincial town.
Abstraction starts to fade.
She's altered me,
Made neuter all the things
That I once felt. And that's
My best (most subtle) but lying
Argument.

There are wars between us
Unfought yet.
Pangs of fate where wind expires.

Where does the bright orange contusion
Lighten, be just a flowery smudge
On the face of a clown?
Sweet, fine applications of gloss
Mature her lips,
But the horizon dims
In English evening rain
Like a screaming gang, their clockwork
Switchblades drawn in chilly Twickenham.
Paris little different
Under the horseshoe trees
Or the brighter, secretive Metro.

From Pandora's panoply of spirits,
Bores and escapades, coins and movies—
Children . . . there is the grime.
The chrome hubcap lost on a street
Hemmed by crumbled flats
Under false gray sky.
The move is made too soon
On the board of reconstruction
That captions articles of speech.
Mixed multitudes are forced
So as to spare the others
Whose goodwill is seen as "mere" charity.
The film's immortalized, raw, raucous,
Chased down an alley by a red balloon.
Amidst crumbling cobble, asphalt
The city votes it
Site specific art, and with
A generous motion sinks the iron box,
"The mirror," deep in concrete.

Titillations themselves
Abominate the play: the phantom face
Of a snowman shining in the sunlight.
Naked memories of blood and straw
Where a scarecrow marks the spot.

Kids play in a nasty puddle.
The actress, Nathalie Baye, perks up
The pages of the Paris Match.
We miss the cognate wheels,
Giant cogs,
Turning in the world's misled mind,
Maltreatment forming every kind of con.
The leering fire truck lurches
Toward battle,
Knight draws his sword.
Victory in history's blunted page?

And death,
Spitting vomit in a world of men.
Ballerinas are inhaled in every breath
Of the enthralled rapist
Like bacteria eating his lungs.
Loud apartment, mother, sisters,
A hand over his eyes to cover
Dirt and empty image.
The Bible falls apart
Beside his smelly bed.
In mourning, a motorcycle boot
Kick starts his mix of dreams.
Arab fish assault his nose
He attacks the swarm
Of disease infected non-native
Flies who he says, "Are no patriots."
Black specks rub off the half-eaten
Angel of his lungs
That are displayed turning
Like a mannequin
In a night store window.

The boy playing the piano
Is afraid.
He sees a man
Breaking the paper,

Climbing naked from la lune.

Moulds of black plastic
Flow from the wall
Of the new museum of art
Reminding us of toxic fumes
And the twin ululating
Lips of sex constrained.
A crude, realistic "dildo"
A la Linda Benglis
Is mined with greased, inflated veins.

We swear to you this is neon truth,
Twang audible in
The march into the showers.

Displayed quilt of memories
Divide girl, woman
Like Lake Ponchartrain runs in
The city of New Orleans
Which snakes through the mist
Above its waters.
Fog rises off the cool, suburban
Beast, glittering with small extended
Strings of light.
Morning shakes off its tight-limbed scales,
Black mass of hair, drying
In the bone parlor of forgetfulness.

Templates of astonished wisdom
Define the forger's craft:
The Versailles Audubon
Of Far Hills, Jersey
Spots video screens in TriBeCa
SoHo on which a redbird combs
Its hair by the installed plaster
Stairs: universal descent
Through tone rows of empty water:

The preening girl,
And then the naked couple fondling
In the basement gallery of the loft.

DALKEY ARCHIVE PAPERBACKS

NICHOLAS MOSLEY, *Accident.*
   Assassins.
   Children of Darkness and Light.
   Impossible Object.
   Judith.
   Natalie Natalia.
WARREN F. MOTTE, *Oulipo.*
YVES NAVARRE, *Our Share of Time.*
WILFRIDO D. NOLLEDO, *But for the Lovers.*
FLANN O'BRIEN, *At Swim-Two-Birds.*
   The Dalkey Archive.
   The Hard Life.
   The Poor Mouth.
FERNANDO DEL PASO, *Palinuro of Mexico.*
RAYMOND QUENEAU, *The Last Days.*
   Pierrot Mon Ami.
REYOUNG, *Unbabbling.*
JULIÁN RÍOS, *Poundemonium.*
JACQUES ROUBAUD,
   The Great Fire of London.
   The Plurality of Worlds of Lewis.
   The Princess Hoppy.
LEON S. ROUDIEZ, *French Fiction Revisited.*
SEVERO SARDUY, *Cobra* and *Maitreya.*
ARNO SCHMIDT, *Collected Stories.*
   Nobodaddy's Children.
JUNE AKERS SEESE,
   Is This What Other Women Feel Too?
   What Waiting Really Means.
VIKTOR SHKLOVSKY, *Theory of Prose.*
CLAUDE SIMON, *The Invitation.*
GILBERT SORRENTINO, *Aberration of Starlight.*
   Imaginative Qualities of Actual Things.
   Mulligan Stew.
   Pack of Lies.
   The Sky Changes.
   Splendide-Hôtel.
   Steelwork.
   Under the Shadow.

W. M. SPACKMAN, *The Complete Fiction.*
GERTRUDE STEIN, *The Making of Americans.*
   A Novel of Thank You.
ALEXANDER THEROUX, *The Lollipop Trollops.*
ESTHER TUSQUETS, *Stranded.*
LUISA VALENZUELA, *He Who Searches.*
PAUL WEST,
   Words for a Deaf Daughter and *Gala.*
CURTIS WHITE,
   Memories of My Father Watching TV.
   Monstrous Possibility.
DOUGLAS WOOLF, *Wall to Wall.*
PHILIP WYLIE, *Generation of Vipers.*
MARGUERITE YOUNG, *Angel in the Forest.*
   Miss MacIntosh, My Darling.
LOUIS ZUKOFSKY, *Collected Fiction.*
SCOTT ZWIREN, *God Head.*

Dalkey Archive Press
ISU Box 4241, Normal, IL 61790–4241
fax (309) 438–7422
Visit our website at www.cas.ilstu.edu/english/dalkey/dalkey.html

DALKEY ARCHIVE PAPERBACKS